T0354642

Writin' the *Range*

JANICE N. CHAPMAN

iUniverse

WRITIN' THE RANGE

iUniverse books may be ordered through booksellers or by contacting:

iUniverse
1663 Liberty Drive
Bloomington, IN 47403
www.iuniverse.com
1-800-Authors (1-800-288-4677)

ISBN: 978-1-5320-5046-6 (sc)
ISBN: 978-1-5320-5048-0 (hc)
ISBN: 978-1-5320-5047-3 (e)

Library of Congress Control Number: 2018908750

Print information available on the last page.

iUniverse rev. date: 09/26/2018

Contents

God's Cowboy

When God sat down and looked upon
The world that he had spun,
He told Himself, "Just one more thing,"
Before His work was done.

We all know how He made Adam,
And then how He made Eve.
But when she later turned to sin—
Oh, how our Lord did grieve!

"I'll make myself a special man,
A man who'll bring me joy,
And I'll give to him an honor code
And call him my cowboy.

"And to this cowboy I'll give a steed,
To help him through his day.
I'll beautify the wide-open spaces,
Where he'll feel free to pray.

"He'll be a breed most looked up to
By others near and far.
By day he'll work beneath the sun;
By night, beneath the stars.

I'll give him wisdom as I see fit,
And common sense as well.
Patience, endurance, and faith in Me,
In My cowboy will always dwell.

He'll delight My soul when he finds
A needful time to pray—
And when he kneels upon My prairies,
I'll listen to what he'll say.

For yes, I'll make Myself a cowboy—
He'll be a breed apart.
And he'll have a special place
Within his Master's heart."

Ken

I watched him walk into the yard.
He was walkin' kind of slow.
He was just a skinny youngster,
But he was one I didn't know.

Shirtsleeves rolled to his elbows,
Jeans and shoes both well worn.
He tended to look around the place
With an expression somewhat forlorn.

I said hello as he came up to me,
And offered a semblance of a grin.
He asked if I had some work for him to do,
And I bade him, "Come on in."

"Fifteen," he said, although I hadn't asked.
Probably a couple of years younger, I don't know.
I asked him if he was hungry,
As his gauntness seemed to show.

I watched him put away a meal
In a way that told me I was right.
Then I caught myself offering the kid
A place to spend the night.

Well, morning came and chores were done;
The boys just took him in.
I didn't know for a week or more
That the youngster's name was Ken.

The men and horses took to him,
And he was kind of handy to have around.
Some months later I realized
The kid had been working for his found.

I don't know why it took so long,
But it dawned on me one day:
This kid had worked his heart out,
And he'd never asked for pay.

I figured up what I owed him,
And I wrote him out a check.
I offered it to him with an apology.
He grinned and said, "No sweat."

I couldn't have asked for a better hand
Than this kid who'd wandered in.
And I've been thankful every day
That the good Lord sent me Ken.

Us Old Cowhands

The kid was green, and we all knew
He was trying to make his place.
Us old cowhands knew the score.
We'd all been there one time too.

Us old cowhands knew the score,
And we'd all help him to learn.
But a place among us
Was something he'd have to earn.

Proving he had what it took
To make a cowhand was a must.
And he'd have to pass the test
To work with the rest of us.

He drew all the jobs
That tested his every skill,
And even I have to admit—
Some of those jobs seemed unreal.

Making a cowhand here
From green was pretty tough.
There was a lot to learn,
And we hoped he had the stuff.

One morn he'd rise a full-blown man,
Thanks to all of us.
Or, if he couldn't cowboy up,
We'd all see his dust.

Emitt

Emitt scrubbed his whiskered jaw,
And shook out his best duds.
Once he'd donned his finest suit,
He soaked his "ever' days" in suds.

Then he caught his roan,
For he was going to town.
And once his "ever' days" were hung to dry,
He tightened the cinches down.

Emitt never knew a girl—
Besides those in the bars, anyway.
But every trip to town Emitt fell in love—
Enough to last to the next payday.

And around the campfire the tales he told
Were of blondes, brunettes, and redheads.
And every payday brought brand-new tales,
On which his dream world fed.

It didn't matter the color of her eyes
Or the swaying of her hips.
It didn't even matter the size of her breasts—
Just the sweetness of her lips.

We laughed with Emitt every night
As he took up our time
To tell us of his latest love—
In details he'd designed!

It gave relief to the same old tales
That normally get told,
As we sat around the campfire listening,
With our coffee getting cold.

Branded

The cow, she balked at the cattle chute.
She wanted not to put herself in.
But a touch from Jacob's prodding stick
Changed her mind right then.

She wasn't through. She tossed her head;
Her horns caught on either side—
Her means of telling us where to go,
And of salvaging her pride.

Another prod, and she went in,
Her opinion loud and clear.
Lonnie caught her head up front,
And Bob closed up the rear.

Shelton had the branding iron:
Its tip a white-hot glow.
What happened next, as he approached,
None of us really know.

But as quickly as the iron touched her side,
Shelton landed on the ground.
And Shelton did not brand the cow—
It was the other way around!

Somehow her hind leg caught
The iron he held right square.
It tipped back against his neck,
And left its imprint there.

We got her leg uncaught
From the side of the branding chute.
And Bob put the brand on her,
And cut her horns to boot.

Shelton's neck healed in time,
And we've all laughed about his plight.
Given how that cow branded him,
Bob had to set her right.

But all of us to a man,
When we look at Shelton's scar,
Know that things could have been much worse,
And we thank our lucky star.

Ranch Foreman

Sitting here alone beside the road
As dusk comes riding in
Makes me wonder why I let
My temper take hold of me again.

I gave up a way of life
That I had known for years.
A younger man was chosen to raise
A better brand of steers.

Long years of loyalty dashed
By temperament and pride.
I should still be the foreman
For the brand, I felt inside.

But a fresh young greenhorn kid,
Himself just college green,
Was given full control
Of the ranch and everything.

No college books can teach him
The downside of ranching ways.
There's no way he can do what I've done,
In just a few days.

Computers for the records kept—
I'll go along with that.
But to know all about ranching—
Why, it's just not like that.

No computer can pull a calf
When a cow is needing help.
Nor can it make a steer out of a bull—
Not that electrical whelp!

It can't set post, or build a fence,
Or raise hay for winter feed,
Or break ice upon the pond
In winter when there's a need.

It can't appraise the wildlife
Or hear a turtle dove.
It can't see the beauty of a meadow
Or feel the touch of love.

But old cowboys aren't wanted
Now that computers have come into play.
And the greenhorns that come with 'em
Can't compete—there's just no way.

But the boss chose the greenhorn
To run the ranch his way.
And after years of working there,
I felt I couldn't stay.

The Bunkhouse

There were nights in the bunkhouse
When near the stove we'd pull up a table.
We'd set the lantern where we could see,
And play cards if we were able—

If we weren't down with consumption,
Or suffering a broken limb or two.
On those cold winter nights
There just wasn't much else to do.

Sometimes we'd get to cussing
The hand that had been dealt,
And sometimes it took a fight or two
To get it all beneath our belt.

But most of the time we'd suffer through
And see the game to its end.
And sometimes after payday,
We'd have whiskey, beer, or gin.

But mostly we're just cowpokes
Just having a little evening fun
To relieve the tensions of the day
In the bunkhouse when the day is done.

Cattle-Moving Day

The sun that parched the prairie grass
Burned down upon the cattle's backs,
And broiled us and our saddled stock
As we tried hard to pick up their tracks

On the hardened ground and sunbaked tufts
Of grass that mostly broke beneath a critter's weight.
But we had to get them moved,
And so such was our fate.

To ride amid the sweltering heat
On this breezeless summer day,
We bunched the cattle that we had,
Then went for the ones that had gone astray.

The perspiration soaked our clothes
And also soaked our mounts.
And with the sun, as it was, beaming down,
We finally had our counts.

The critters fought us all the way
To the corrals. We put them in,
A bawling, milling, sweating herd,
And sweating, weary mounts and men.

We all saw to our horses then
And cooled each one of them out.
We'll need them again tomorrow;
Of that there is no doubt.

Then weary, smelly, dust-caked men
Sought the cooling water trough,
Where we could bathe and cool down a bit
And get the day's stench off.

Tomorrow will be another day,
But at least the cattle are in.
And tomorrow morn before we start,
We'll run the count again.

Quicksand

We were bringing in the horses,
My neighbor, Gary, and me.
Things were going pretty good,
Until one yearling filly broke free.

Champion and I turned with her
As she broke away.
We had to turn her back.
We couldn't let her go astray.

But then she crossed the creek,
And things got out of hand:
My paint had closed the distance,
But he ran into quicksand.

He screamed out in panic,
And I had to yell and hope.
But Gary somehow heard me,
And came back swinging his rope.

For the first time in his life,
His rope sailed straight and true.
It landed over Champ and me,
Just like we needed it to.

Champion was thrashing around in panic,
And we were sinking fast.
Even I could not get free:
The quicksand has us both in its grasp.

But it wasn't until after
He got his feet on solid ground
That Gary and I together
Finally got Champion settled down.

We cleaned the saddle with sage.
We did the best we could.
The saddle would have to be cleaned and soaped;
That was totally understood.

But then we decided to let her go,
The filly that had gone astray.
We took the rest of the herd of horses in.
We'd had enough for one day.

The Army Mule

We had to break some army mules
For the army, so Dad said.
For every one we broke for them,
They'd pay us by the head.

Most of them weren't too bad;
They broke in like they should.
It just took a few long weeks
To teach them what we could.

But now and then there came along
A mule we called "Ole Red"
Who wasn't going to break at all,
No matter what we did.

He bit and stomped and reared, and shied
From everything we tried to do.
He took pure delight in doing his best
To destroy everything he could too.

We finally ran him into the corral
Where we broke young wild colts in.
We tied him to the snubbing post
And let him hit the lasso's end.

He swapped ends a time or two.
I thought he'd break his neck.
But he finally broke the rope instead,
And left the corral a total wreck.

He brayed his cussing long and loud
For all the range to hear.
That he'd be old before he broke
Was my greatest fear.

A special crew was brought in
To break this mule, Ole Red.
I thought they'd starve him plumb to death;
He was the only one that wasn't fed.

It took an awful lot of time
For that mule to finally give in.
And I'm not sure who cussed the most—
That goldarn mule or the men.

The Last Cattle Drive

I think I knew before he left on the drive
That he'd not come home alive.
He hugged me to his cowboy breast
A few moments before he joined the rest.

I thought for a moment that I saw a tear in his eye,
But out in these parts cowboys don't cry.
Finally he whispered in a voice so low,
"Whether I'll make it back or not, I don't know."

Cattle get strange when they're trailin'
In territories strange and new.
Any strange sound, or the sound of a gun,
Is a good enough reason for the cattle to run.

There's rivers and thickets and sudden ravines,
And prairie dog holes that are often unseen.
A knife will slit the throat of a downed cow or horse,
And we may well eat them for the evening course.

Dangers come from everywhere,
And we all must do what must be done,
From killing rustlers who try to steal,
To helping Cookie fix a broken wagon wheel.

Weather and storms all add to the cost,
After which some of us are invariably lost.
Don't cry for me, Sis, if I don't come home.
Remember, I didn't make this drive alone.

Some of us won't come home alive,
But we're making this last cattle drive.
It must have been something he'd felt inside.
We lost him and his horse on that last drive.

Cookie's Last Meal

Ole Cookie'd ridden on ahead.
He'd find a place to rest
And fix us all a bite to eat,
Though his cooking wasn't the best.

We ate dust all afternoon,
And fought the wind as well.
It'd be a while before we could
Alight and rest a spell.

It's bad enough on a long day's ride
When we only get a breeze,
And when the cattle that we drive
Aren't as spooky as some of these.

I hadn't known the wind to gale
Like this in many years.
It was tough to keep in line
These few hundred head of steers.

The cattle bawled as we pushed them on.
Some tried to turn an' break.
They kept us busy every minute.
My limbs began to ache.

At last the shadows lengthened;
We'd get to alight a spell and rest,
And eat some of Cookie's cookin',
Even though it weren't the best.

It looked to us, as we rode in
Expecting to find our evening meal,
That Cookie'd had some bad luck
And had broken a wagon wheel.

We didn't know quite what happened,
But Cookie was lying dead.
But he'd managed before he died
To grip the rattler's head.

We cut the rattler from his hand,
And buried Cookie there.
We fixed the broken wagon wheel,
And the rattler we all shared.

It was a somber riding crew
That feasted on Cookie's last meal.
Him giving his life to feed us
Hadn't been a part of the deal.

But ole Cookie'd ridden on ahead
To find a place to rest.
And though the rattler had gotten him,
His last meal was his best.

The Lobo

My horse flicked his ears and snorted,
Turned his head to one side.
I turned in my saddle and looked behind me,
To find we weren't alone on our ride.

A big lobo wolf had joined up with us,
Though he kept a ways behind.
When we stopped, so did he,
Wary of horses and humankind.

Late evening I stopped beside a spring
To water my horse and me,
And I caught that big lobo
Watching from behind a tree.

That night I made camp,
And cooked some vittles too.
The lobo stopped just beyond the light,
But I throwed him a biscuit or two.

Morning found him still there,
Waiting on our sleepy company.
We rode on that day,
The lobo, the horse, and me.

It seemed like everything I did
The lobo had to share.
By the time I reached the ranch,
The lobo was right there.

He'd done no harm to horse or me,
So it seemed only fair
That when we had table scraps,
The lobo got his share.

For several years he hung around.
I came to think of him as a pet.
For sure he wasn't a creature
I'd soon be likely to forget.

But then one morn he was gone;
He'd never touched his pan.
Perhaps he found a mate,
Or is now riding with another horse and man.

Tumbleweeds

I saw that tumbleweed
There against the fence.
It and all its buddies:
A gray line of defense.

Helpless they looked
As they all leaned there.
No more tumbling
To spread their seeds everywhere.

But my eye caught the beauty
Of their intricate design.
So a picture of those tumbleweeds
Soon became mine.

Tumbleweed memories
In some folklore I'd heard,
Even though I must admit,
Some tales seemed pretty absurd.

I'd moved back east
Where the word was unknown.
And I didn't see a tumbleweed again
Until I moved back home.

Somehow they belong to
The legends of the West.
Although what their purpose is,
Is anybody's guess.

Sagebrush

As he rode down from the canyon,
Toward the valley there below,
He smelled the scent of sage—
Oh, how high that sage can grow!

He thought of days he'd swung an axe,
To cut that sagebrush down,
To clear the way for cows to pass
And to graze the grass around.

He thought of the hours he had spent
On the tractor pulling sagebrush roots,
To look again the coming spring
Upon their brand-new shoots.

He remembered, too, the nights there were
That to rub his tired pony down,
Sprigs of cut-up sagebrush
Were the only thing around.

Even in his younger years
At times, he recalled, he'd found
That lying on a bed of sage
Beat lying on the ground.

And in the spring when purple blossoms
Gave forth their scent anew,
He knew he'd always love this land
Where that awesome sagebrush grew.

Ole Cord

Ole Cord was fond of bragging
That he could ride anything alive.
So we decided we'd just see,
And have some fun around this old dive.

Down on Chapman's Range
Lived a tinhorn's special fare:
A kind of four-legged varmint
That around our parts was rare.

So few had ever seen her,
This long-legged rangy mare,
And fewer had caught up to her
On the prairie runnin' fair.

No man had e'er been on her—
We knew that for a fact.
Now we had to figure out
How to get the mare brought back.

We knew she'd surely show Ole Cord
Just exactly what he lacked,
While we had to sit and swallow
His long-jawed bragging as a fact.

We waited until Ole Cord
Was riding line one day
To bring that wild mare in
And put here in our corral to stay.

Ole Cord's eyes just twinkled
When he came in and saw that mare.
"Wal," he said in his gentle drawl,
"What's this you have in here?"

"Aw, we just brought in a new one
We thought you'd like to ride."
Ole Cord gave us an eye ...
I know he knew we lied.

But true to his bragging—
And to all of our surprise—
He roped this mangy wild horse,
And hung onto his prize.

She did some fancy dancing.
The corral filled fast with dust.
Ole Cord talked to her, and as he did,
He forgot the rest of us.

It took almost two months before dawned the day
That we could watch Ole Cord ride.
He'd gentled down that rangy mare,
And he saddled her with pride.

The ride he rode for us was short.
He'd mastered the wildness call.
And now to us his word is fact:
It ain't no brag a'tall.

My Grandson and the Stallion

I woke up this morning
And stretched amid a yawn,
And almost had a heart attack
When I saw what my eyes lit upon.

In the corral with the stallion
I'd bought just yesterday,
My grandson found his legs
A delightful place to play.

As I watched in horror
While the baby played between those legs,
I might as well have been sitting
On a dozen powder kegs!

I could see all kinds of things
That stallion might have done—
If he'd had a mind to—
To my trusting grandson.

From the front legs to the back legs
The toddler stumbled and fell,
And just to break his fall …
He grabbed the stallion's tail!

And he chortled the air with laughter
As between those back legs he fell.
The stallion turned his head,
And I swear he smiled as well.

But he never moved a muscle
As the baby played beneath his might.
And I slowly, breath abated,
Strolled toward the unlikely sight.
I knew deep down inside
Sudden moves I shouldn't dare,
As I slowly inched my way
Toward that unlikely pair.

The baby absently moved away,
And the stallion followed him.
He fondled the baby's face
And snickered softly to him.

The baby laughed and petted
That soft muzzle close to him,
And those tiny fingers on his hands
Found the mane of his newfound friend.

I froze as the stallion turned him
Toward the gate he'd gone through,
And then nudged him gently
To get him to come back through.

I picked up my grandson,
Relieved no harm had come to him,
And said my thanks to the stallion
That he'd turned out to be a friend.

Old Blossom's Foal

"Hey! C'mere! C'mere!" she cried out
As she raced to my side.
"Later," said I, as she tugged at my jeans;
But she'd not be denied.

"Ya gotta come see!" she exclaimed,
Tugging at me to follow her back
To the barn, where the stall for the mare
Was the first past the tack.

"Look!" she cried out
As we neared the enclosure.
"Old Blossom's got a baby!"
And she did have for sure.

A fine handsome foal
Of a lineage a way back.
And the darkest of colors:
A pure satin black.

But Old Blossom was too old
To give me a foal.
Yet here in her stall
Was a babe of black coal.

She should have been up,
The colt by her side.
But Old Blossom was still.
Old Blossom had died.

An orphan she'd left
As she passed from this earth,
Having died shortly after
She'd given birth.

We'd have to feed him by hand
For quite a few days,
Until he was some older
And able to graze.

I explained all of this
To the child by my side,
And I felt terribly helpless
As she sat down and cried.

Old Blossom was a pet
And had stolen her heart.
She'd never given a thought
To her and Old Blossom apart.

"What will you name him?"
This I asked of her.
She'd want to feed him;
Of that I was sure.

She wiped away tears,
And gave a sniffle or two.
"I'll just call him Midnight.
I guess that'll do."

"That'll do just fine," said I to her,
As her arms closed around him.
And her love then transferred
From Old Blossom to him.

The Little Cowpoke

He stood beside his steed
And waited for his call,
And then he rode that bucking horse.
Not once did he fall.

He gave it everything he had,
And the crowd cheered him on.
He'd drawn the horse to ride,
The one they called Midnight Dawn.

That horse bucked, and he bucked hard.
He bucked up and down, and to the left and right.
And with a spin he tried to unseat the young cowpoke
Who sat upon his back this night.

The eight-second bell could scarcely be heard
Above the noise of the crowd.
Their cheers and whistles told the little cowpoke
That of him they were proud.

When the cheering quit,
He felt no remorse.
He'd had himself quite a ride
On Midnight Dawn, his favorite stick horse!

His Little Cowboy Boots

The cowboy boots he wore to school
Did so hurt his feet.
And so he took them off
And set them in the aisle beside his seat.

His teacher spotted his cowboy boots
Sitting beside his chair,
And asked of her young pupil
Why he had put them there.

He'd have to wear them during school,
She did explain to him.
And then she helped him tug and pull
To get them on again.

But they still hurt his feet,
And thus he told her so,
Looking at his booted feet,
She discovered that wasn't the way they go.

She helped him pull them off again,
And put the right foot in each boot.
Then she asked him why to kindergarten
He'd worn these tight cowboy boots.

He shrugged and said to her
That his brother's boots they were,
But he had to have a pair to wear
In front of the other kids and her.

With the boots in place once more,
The teacher had a thought.
She asked of this young pupil,
"Where are the mittens that you brought?"

And the answer he proudly gave her
Shook the teacher to her roots.
He calmly replied,
"They're in the toes of my boots!"

Proud Grandma

"Rocky 'orse, G'amma," he said
As he crawled up on my lap.
We rocked a little while,
And then he took a nap.

"Me wanna pony, G'amma.
Me wanna pony too."
With smiling eyes I said,
"I'll see what I can do."

"Can you talk to Gran'pa, G'amma,
And see if I can have a baby 'orse?"
As I looked into those eyes,
I answered him, "Of course."

His Grandpa balked a bit at that,
But it seemed he understood.
He came up with a gentle colt,
Said, "You'd better treat it good."

How proud my grandson was that day
When he rode the colt for the first time!
I knew right then that from that point on
He'd proudly call him "mine."

He learned to ride and rope,
And cut and brand as well—
And how to sort the cattle out
That Grandpa wanted to sell.

His grandpa taught him everything
A grandson had to know.
A better cowboy you've yet to meet,
And Grandpa will proudly tell you so.

Now the years have come and gone,
Yet when my grandson wants things done,
With a twinkle in his eye
To his grandma he will come.

He knows full well his grandma
Will do his bidding every time.
For he doesn't just have her number—
He has her tied in binder twine!

The Rodeo Rider

If I get away with a few scrapes and bruises,
And if a little bit of pride is all this rider loses;
If I come away from my ride with no broken bones,
And I can miss the hospital on my way home;

If I can ride that bull—the meanest of the lot
And the bell catches me on the ground not,
Then I can hooray for me and my time,
Because I'm not young. I'm almost in my prime.

If the young horse can reach new ways in the sky,
Or give me new memories about which I can lie,
Then I'll feel I've succeeded as I lie on the ground,
To be helped to my feet by the rodeo clown.

If the steer I've just bulldogged to the ground
Bruises my legs by his sheer weight and pounds;
If a bone isn't broken, then I'll be glad
I'm teamed with the best partner I've ever had.

If the wild cow kicks and I lose a little skin,
I'll be more determined to get that bottled milk then.
And though I may lose when the judges call "out,"
It'll give me something to run my jaw about.

If my rope has a bad day in the calf-roping event,
And my piggin' string breaks because it's too spent,
I'll curse the bad luck that befell me this day,
And I'll buy me some new ones the next time I see pay.

But whichever way I come out in the end,
I'll be thankful for a good horse, and those I call friend.
And every time I'm asked if I had fun on the tour,
I'll smile, and I'll answer that question with "Sure!"

Stay Out of My Wheat Fields

"Stay out of my wheat fields!"
Our dad used to say.
But when he wasn't looking,
We rode through them anyway.

"You'll tear my wheat out by the roots.
You'll ruin my growing crop!
And this riding through my wheat fields,
I tell you girls, had better stop!"

He let the cattle graze in the winter months
While the wheat was young and green.
And to us, keeping the horses off
Just didn't mean a thing.

It was fun to chase each other;
Off through the fields we'd go.
We knew we'd get punished.
That didn't bother us, though.

We spent hours in the wheat fields
Clearing ground for grain,
Cursing hot and humid air,
And wishing it would rain.

When golden grains of amber
Waved gently during June,
We knew that the combines
Would be rolling soon.

We knew then that our fun
Would have to wait awhile.
And we'd remember our dad's voice,
And then we'd have to smile.

"Stay out of my wheat fields!"
We'd hear our daddy say.
And we knew that he knew
We rode in them anyway.

Old Barns

How awesome that they've stood
And passed the test of time.
How beautiful they must have been
When they were in their prime.

How many hands did it take
To cut and trim the wood
And peg or nail each and every board
And make sure it fit the way it should?

How many dreams were cast aloft
With each new barn they built?
How many hours did it take
To make it solid so it wouldn't tilt?

How many farm folk and cowboys
Have spent their nights inside,
Either just for a place to sleep
Or to doctor animals that might have later died?

How many animals have the old barns sheltered
Against the years of weather of all kind?
How many shocks of feed or bales of hay
Could one in their lofts still find?

How many kids had happy hours
While playing in those old barns?
How many of them listen now
To us old folks telling yarns

Of how we used to shuck the corn,
And the hours we went through,
To have us tell them how later on that night,
"We enjoyed the old barn dances too"?

Oh yes, they've had their places,
Down through our history.
Although all that came their way
Was not always pleasantries.

They knew their share of burnings,
And gunplay as it were,
And other grievous crimes
That old barns sometimes lure.

Though now the wood is splintered
And most has turned to gray,
Those old barns were important parts
Of living in their day.

But to see those old barns now
In various stages of disrepair
Still brings to mind fond memories
That some of us still share.

Dust Storms

Plowed fields are the greatest thing
Dust devils have found as a playing norm.
They twirl and skip and tease the air
That blows them into the life they form.

And they grow into great clouds of dust
That settles upon everything,
There's not a thing that they neglect
As the silt sifts and clings.

As the wind picks up
And the storm becomes full-blown,
It becomes a million specks of dust
That blast you to the bone.

They cake upon a sweaty face,
Become mud wiped upon a sleeve.
And woe to the gal with the hardwood floor,
As the dust will cling and cleave!

It stings your eyes, it burns your nostrils,
It clogs your lungs inside.
There's no place to get away from it;
There's just no place to hide.

'Kerchiefs around your nose
Are a temporary relief.
At least it helps to keep the sand out,
And helps to let you breathe.

Your shoes for your own bare feet
Surely seem a fair and decent trade,
When the sand finds its way inside your socks
And blisters toes that inside your shoes do wade.

Neither a drink of water nor a plate of food
Is safe from the sandstorm's blast.
You spit the sand from the food you eat,
And wipe the film from the water inside your glass.

The sheets are filled with bits of sand,
Though the bed was fully made.
And you'll shake the sheets to rid the sand,
Before to all "good night" you bade.

But it'll be back the morrow morn
To plague your coming day,
And haunt you again throughout your wake
Just like it did today.

The Lure of the Desert

The lure of the desert
Does call us back home.
We wander across it,
Mostly and nearly always alone.

It cooks us until
We're past being well done.
It parches our throats
With its hot desert sun.

The desert is where man and beast
Travel at night or early in the dawn
And hope the waterholes
Haven't dried up and gone.

It's where the shifting sand
Keeps the dunes ever new,
And the wind drives us onward
Until we're weary of it too.

It's where endurance is put
To its very last test,
And survival depends
On a man doing his best.

His rewards are the silence
And the changing of hues,
And peace from within
As he lives with these truths

That are as hard as the rocks
When the mountain slides.
He has his burros to depend on
As his desert guides.

Even with the rattlers
And the scorpions that sting,
There's nothing more beautiful
Than the desert in spring.

And for the man who loves it
And likes traveling alone,
The lure of the desert
Will always call him back home.

Columns of Smoke

The columns of smoke lifted
To become clouds of black,
And he knew before he got there
The fire was in his shack.

It could have been that lightning
Had hit the shack,
Or hit the pile of wood
He had stacked out back.

The closer he rode,
The larger seemed the flames.
And he knew before he reached the blaze
All that it had claimed.

Not much he could say
Had e'er belonged to him.
But what little he owned
Held sentiment deep within.

For though he lived here alone
With his possessions so few,
It was still the only home
This cowboy'd ever knew.

His ma had died when he was young,
And his pa was later laid to rest.
The shack with its belongings
Was all he possessed.

Now weather took its lasting toll;
His home stood there no more.
It had burned like dry kindling wood,
The fire even burning out the floor.

He watched the flames in silence,
Feeling helpless through and through.
He felt the tears well up in his eyes;
He'd lost the only home he knew.

He watched the smoldering embers
With an emptiness inside.
It almost seemed demeaning
That back to this he'd had to ride.

A new house he would build
With timbers fresh and new.
A handsome thing it would be
When he at last was through.

It wouldn't replace the memories
That lay smoldering here—
The memories of his childhood
That would always be so dear.

But he'd build a brand-new shelter
In the place where he lived alone,
And build a place for his pony
On that place they both called home.

What's a Windmill?

"What's a windmill? What does it do?"
The youngster asked of me.
How could I describe that tower
To him just from my memory?

How do I describe the way
They build a windmill tower frame,
Or the wheel turning in the wind,
When I can't even think of its name?

How can I describe the leathers
And how those things work?
Or how the pipe is pulled up and down
To bring the water from beneath the dirt?

How can I describe to him
How the water comes aloft
And pours its sweet goodness
Into the waiting water trough?

How can I describe to him the wailing
The windmill does from time to time,
Sitting alone out on the prairies,
Where its labors run on 24-7 time?

How can I describe the creaking
It does every now and then
As it draws from Mother Earth
Sweet water from deep within?

It runs not on electricity,
Nor does it run on gas.
It's an item nearly forgotten—
A phantom of the past.

Yet now and then you see one,
Sometimes one still at its task.
But how do I describe it
To the youngster who had asked?

As simple as it is in its structure,
And as stately as the windmill stands,
I find it hard to describe
So the youngster will understand.

He'll just have to see one—
And nowadays they are so few!—
Because it's easier to describe them
With one standing in full view.

That's What Us Cowboys Do

I asked him why he drinks,
And why he gambles too.
He twinkled all over and said,
"That's what us cowboys do."

I asked him why he flirted
And seemed not to care
That I was the girl
He had brought there.

His eyes began to sparkle,
And a chuckle came forth too.
He told me not to worry.
Because "that's what us cowboys do."

He told me not to worry,
Said he loved me through and through,
Said he'd always love me,
But "that's just what us cowboys do."

Out on the dance floor,
I in the circle of his arms,
Everything else was lost
To the secret of his charms.

I knew then that I loved him
And that he loved me too.
And it really doesn't matter
What the other cowboys do.

The West Texas Wind

I was asked if I could,
Would I do it all over again?
Would I fall in love with you
In the west Texas wind?

Ah, yes, I would love you
All over again,
While we were blessed
By the west Texas wind.

I would be in your arms
Daytime or night,
Wrapped in your arms
While the wind made it right.

I would be with you always,
And enjoy it again,
The love that we shared
In the west Texas wind.

You now live with God,
But I have memories of when
We shared our love
In the west Texas wind.

Don't Be Accused of Being a Cowboy

Don't be accused of being a cowboy
Just so you'll have something to do.
Because if you're not a true cowboy,
That title will come back to haunt you.

You're young; you're anxious; and you're willing.
And that says a whole lot for you.
But cowboyin's not so easy;
You'll do things you don't want to do.

Like killin' a calf that you've raised, son,
To feed a family at home.
Or sellin' a favorite of your horses
To pay the banker your loan.

Cowboyin's not always pockets that jingle.
Much of it is pain to the bone.
And hunger is often a companion
When the banker refuses your loan.

Life doesn't always play fair, son.
Most times it stomps hard on you.
So don't be accused of being a cowboy
Unless you're sure that's what you want to do.

It's all done differently in the movies,
And most every film turns out right.
But out here in the world of reality,
We shed many tears in our plight.

There's no one to step in with big money
To lift our burdens from us.
We're a breed apart from the others,
But we cowboys all do have a plus.

We're respectful, hard workin', and true,
Every day and with everything that we do.
And never is a job left undone—
A cowboy will always come through.

But take pride in becoming a cowboy,
If you're sure that's what you want to do.
And let me be able to be proud of
The man that I'll see in you.

But if your heart's just not in it,
Then find yourself something other to do.
And don't let the title of Cowboy
Come back in the future to haunt you.

Another Pint of Blood

I gave the waitress my order as she came over near me:
"A hot roast beef—if you have one left—and coffee."
I didn't realize as I sat down in a
booth in the café that day
That I would overhear what two
local cowboys had to say.

Two men sat in a booth nearby
discussing general things,
One in a cowboy hat and mustache,
the other in dirty jeans.
One was evidently paying for the meal for both of them,
Because the other just didn't have the means.

Times are hard, and getting harder by the day.
Realization of that hit home when
I heard one cowboy say:
"I guess I'll go out and sell another pint of blood again.
I'm broke, and there's no money coming in."

There are places here that offer a T-shirt, a five, or a ten.
But you have to wait a month to return to them.
Unwanted T-shirts are gathered in a different stack,
And are given then to charity—they're never taken back.

"Calves," he said, "aren't ready to sell,
and the pickup needs some gas.
Things just aren't like they were a few weeks before last.
Times are getting harder, and harder by the day.
I need to sell another pint of blood today.

"I sold a pint last week when the
wife asked me for money,
And when I told her I'd be right back,
she looked at me kind of funny.
I never told her I'd sold my blood
so she could feed the kids.
She'd probably be mad at me if she
knew that's what I did.

"How I'll get by these next few weeks
is something I don't know.
Maybe I won't run out of blood
before my crops can grow."
I sat there in silence as I listened to the man,
And I knew full well a man will do what he can.

With times being hard, and getting harder by the day,
A working, struggling cowboy
will somehow find a way.
And when it comes to sacrificing
for the family that he loves,
A cowboy will cowboy up and sell
another pint of blood.

I'm a Meat-and-Potatoes Man

I want all of you to know,
And to likewise understand,
That I'm just an ordinary person,
But I'm a meat-and-potatoes man.

Everything I like to eat
Can be grown on my own land.
Potatoes come from my own fields,
And beef from my own brand.

I may rise before daylight,
And my days may be hard and long,
But meat and potatoes will soothe my ache,
Even when my day goes wrong.

I don't want any fancy food
Placed upon my plate,
Just good old meat and potatoes;
The rest will have to wait.

And when it comes my time
To lie beneath that hardened clay,
Carved in the stone above
The grave in which I'll lay,

I'd sure like to know
That my epitaph will say,
"He was a meat-and-potatoes man
To the end of his last day."

To Dream Another Time

He leaned back on the shade tree,
His arms upon his knees.
His mind wandered into dreamland
As he soaked up the summer breeze.

At fourteen he was too young,
He'd heard the grown-ups say,
To do the kind of work required
To earn some decent pay.

The little jobs he'd done in town,
Like cleaning out the stable,
Didn't pay him very much, but still,
They helped his mom keep food upon the table.

The dreams he dreamed
On these warm summer days
Were all of a better life,
One with better living ways.

His mind allowed him to dream
Of vast uncounted grassy acres.
His cattle were his, all free of debt.
There were no troublesome bankers.

His pony was the finest mount,
And swift upon its feet.
And he smiled at the golden acres
Of ripening golden wheat.

But then his mother called to him,
Said it was suppertime.
And so he tucked away his dreams
To dream another time.

Champ

I sat myself in the saddle
And swayed with every step.
And Champ's head bobbed up and down
With the rhythm that he kept.

Ah, cattle! He could work them!
That was something that he knew.
But on his list of priorities,
It was low down—something he didn't like to do.

He could cut with the best of them,
And bring back that straying cow.
But some days he'd rather act dumb
And pretend he didn't know how.

If you could catch the heels with your rope,
He'd quickly take out the slack,
And that calf would not get up
So long as he could back.

I've praised him many times
While out there on the trail.
That paint horse had a lot of stamina
Tucked between his head and tail.

Put him with another horse
And he'd show you what was where;
And you'd best be planted on his back
If you planned to stay up there.

No, he wasn't a show horse;
He was as ugly as they come.
But he didn't like working cattle.
He'd much rather play dumb.

But then I thought about him,
And somehow I know it's true.
He liked hearing human voices,
And his playing dumb extracted words from me too.

He liked being talked to,
But usually we had no time.
We needed him to work cattle,
Sometimes turning on a dime.

He liked being number one.
He was that self-centered too.
But he could be the dumbest thing on four legs
When he wanted to.

Then in the next instant,
As a cow horse he was the best.
I just never knew which way he'd act,
And I never dared to guess.

But smart he was, I must confess,
Though he was ornery as could be.
And I know he dreamed up things to do
Just so he could laugh at me.

He'd work with me all day long,
Or work against me just as hard.
But still there's not another living thing
I'd rather have as my pard.

He didn't just leave memories;
He left behind a legacy.
And I hope he's in horse heaven,
Where all good horses ought to be.

Hit by Lightning

I remember well the evening
The storm was closing in;
The cow had left her calf out in the pasture,
And I had to go bring it in.

Lightning streaked and played
Against a purple sky.
To find a calf amid ravine and sage
Was what I had to try.

We were halfway to the pasture,
My horse Champ and I,
When lightning hit my Champion
Right above his left eye.

How long the storm raged around us
Neither of us knew,
For my horse lay there beside me
When I finally came to.

I carried his hoofprint
On my leg for a week or so.
He had stepped on my leg getting up;
He hadn't meant to though.

How I got up on his bare back,
I'll never really know.
I guess he must have knelt
For me to get on him just so.

We never did find the calf
We had started to look for that night.
The lightning blinded my horse,
And it shook me up too that night.

I don't know how long it was
That we had to wait before Dad found me
Draped over Champion's withers
There by the corral gate.

The Blizzard

The wind swept the swirling snow
Across the lone highway.
I hadn't seen it play and swirl
Since I had moved away.

I could not see the landscape
Because everything was covered in white,
Except for my car, from which I viewed
This panoramic evening sight.

A beautiful thing to behold,
As in front of me the blizzard swept.
But I knew of many other blizzards
My memory had kept,

Some that raged on for days on end
When the cattle bunched against the cold.
And not getting to them with cake and hay
Left many a nightmare to unfold.

Many an empty table has been set
While the blinding blizzards raged.
And just like the herds that died,
Some people themselves became crazed.

The bills they owed would still come due,
In spite of the blizzard's paradox.
And they'd lose everything they hoped to own
With the dying off of their stock.

Many tears have followed the heels
Of the winter blizzards that have come to play.
I thought of the heartaches in its wake
As I watched the snow swirl and play.

The Old Cowboy

I saw this man I've known for years,
Yet seeing him almost brought me tears.
I couldn't tell you how many miles
He's ridden the range, with all its trials.

Or how many years it took the wind
To carve the wrinkles in his facial skin.
The twinkling eyes I used to see
No longer twinkled merrily.

A voice so soft and baritone
That took the weariness from bone
No longer came out soft and clear
The way it did in yesteryear.

No songs now came out to play
To sing our weary blues away.
No whistled tunes will I now hear,
Which used to fill the air so clear.

For now his breathing comes in gasps,
And his voice is now a thinning rasp.
His smile no longer finds its place
Amid the worry on his face.

His legs are bent—and yes, are bowed—
From the years of horses that he rode.
But when it's mentioned that's what he used to do,
He makes the comment, "Yeah, I've rode a few."

His legs no longer dance to tune and rhyme
The way they did once upon a time.
His left hand is bent and filled with pain
From the years he rode and held the rein.

The hand that used to hold the girls on the dance floor
Is a hand he feels he can use no more.
And in spite of the ranges on which he's been,
His body is a vessel, now frail and thin.

He was a man who shouldered life day by day
And handled whatever came his way.
He helped his mother until she died,
And then with an older son's pride

He took his handicapped brother under his wing
And treated him first in everything.
He did his best as a big brother to see
That happy his younger brother would be.

And though it pained him to go and do,
He always saw his younger brother through.
Brotherly love was unsurpassed
In this old cowboy who can barely gasp.

And it saddens me that I had to see
A man who's been a friend to me
In a situation where I cannot help, yet I know
It won't be long before he'll go.

We'll miss him here on earth.
I guess we all know this cowboy's worth.
But God will gain on heaven's row
The best cowhand He'll ever know.

Zeke's Going Home

He sat there swirling coffee grounds
Around the bottom of his cup,
Wondering if he'd done the right thing
With the life he'd given up.

As he watched the coffee grounds settle
To the bottom of the cup again,
Thoughts of what he'd left behind
Came back to him again.

He'd left a home of comfort,
And a struggling mom and dad.
He was one less mouth to feed
Of the seven that they had.

Luck just wasn't with his dad;
Farming was not his heartfelt thing.
And the livelihood got harder
As each new baby came into being.

Zeke had finally come of age.
He could work like any man could.
He decided that by leaving home to work,
He could help them when he could.

The years dragged on by,
And Zeke grew older still.
Cowboy life was all he knew.
But thoughts of home fortified his will.

Thoughts of how his mom might look,
Or how bent his dad might be.
How many kids they'd had in all,
Some whom he had yet to see.

He took another swallow,
Then splashed the rest into the fire.
He guessed it was time to go now
And follow up his desire.

He saddled his favorite gelding,
And bade the crew goodbye.
Home was calling Zeke again.
He heard its inward cry.

Good Ole Oklahoma

Here's to good ole Oklahoma,
With her pastures sweet and green,
which are brushed with gentle breezes
That are felt instead of seen.

With her hills of awesome beauty,
And her twisters often mean.
Where the paths of her twisters
Can be counted on each spring.

We have our wind and dust storms,
But we have something more:
We have a state full of good people,
Though some of us are poor.

Good ole Oklahoma offered talent
On those old-time movie screens.
And if we don't remember all the others,
We all remember Gene.

An airport, a museum, and streets
With his name are forever teamed.
Will Rogers paid us honor
With his talent and his dreams.

And even Miss America
Lent us one of her crowns
When Laverne's Jane Jayroe made Miss America
In the 1967 countdowns.

There are poets bred and raised here
On ole Oklahoma's back,
Though one of them is known more so than others,
The man we know as Baxter Black.

Our sports are not to be outdone;
Our teams are some of the best.
Oklahoma may not be that large,
But she's the pearl of the Midwest.

Cattle roam the ranges
For rodeos, beef, and hide.
And unmatched anywhere
Is an Okie rancher's pride.

Horses are grown for quality,
Even out on the track.
But mostly they're bred for ridin',
Either saddled or bareback.

Dogs we raise for breeders,
Some for roundin' cattle too.
Some just for the little ones,
And some for blind folk too.

We host some good musicians.
They'll play for you to dance.
And if you want to join in,
Most will give you a chance.

Museums dot our cities
With our western folklore too.
There's not much you can find in Oklahoma
That our people cannot do.

Oklahoma by Night

I asked Uncle Joe where he'd been.
It was already morning
And I hadn't seen him come in.

There in the corral stood a beautiful bay,
I wouldn't have noticed it,
Except I heard it neigh.

There were other nights
When Uncle Joe left home
Just as evening ran out of daylight.

A different horse now and then
He brought home when he came in.
I never thought about where he'd been.

A horse only stayed a day or two,
Then Uncle Joe would turn up
With one that was new.

He seemed to have buyers
Every time he came in,
And he fell in line with the best of the liars.

When my curiosity finally set in,
I asked Uncle Joe
Just where he had been.

"Oklahoma by night is a place I do well.
That's where I get these horses
I bring home and sell."

I couldn't argue about what I didn't know.
I learned in later years about
Where my uncle would go.

I didn't want to believe Uncle Joe would steal;
But I learned it was fact—
"Oklahoma by night" was indeed very real.

The Auction

They ragged him about his bet
On the colt there in the ring:
The young yearling stud colt
That to him would mean everything.

His bid was twenty-five dollars,
And that was his last cent,
Even though the friends around him
Teased him about what he'd spent.

And on a horse he'd have to wait
Another year to train and ride.
His want for that young stud colt
Was a yearning deep inside.

"I need a horse," I heard him say,
"And by the time he's big enough to ride,
I'll know him and he'll know me."
He spoke with love and pride.

I knew the colt would have a home.
I didn't have to think about it twice.
I told the auctioneer to let
The kid have him for that price.

The colt's name was Nickles,
And still is, though he's now turned bay—
A loving gentle stud colt
Sharing his boy every day.

Old-Time Cowboys

I never lived in days of old
Where cowboys rode the range,
And often rode it alone
Into territories new and strange,

Where they met each moment
With the best of what they had each day—
And never knew when they'd be attacked
By an injured or loco'd stray.

Where fence posts didn't dot the land
With barbed wire to bar the way;
Where a man could ride in any direction,
Or on any piece of land could stay;

Where prayer might be at the water's edge,
Where the banks threatened to overflow—
Or again during a summer drought
When the water was really low.

Where home might be, and often was,
A stand of pinon trees;
Where a man prayed for summer breeze,
Or in the winter that he'd not freeze;

Where his clothes might be skinned out hide,
And his shoes might be the same,
And where bullets were too expensive
For him not to take accurate aim.

Where jobs were few, pay was low,
And food was not the best,
But in my heart I have a place
For those cowboys who tamed the West.

The Night Wind

I woke up with a start.
The night wind had an eerie sound.
My horse was nervous, too,
And prancing all around.

And I knew if I was going with him,
I'd best get off the ground.
I grabbed my hat and saddle.
He shivered as his back the saddle found.

Not one moment too soon
Did up on his back I climb.
He was off into the night,
And he was running record time.

He clamped down on the bit
And paid no attention to the reins.
He might as well have had wings
As he sped across the plains.

Every time the wind let out
That eerie, mournful moan,
It scared the horse a little more.
That horse was going home.

I was glad I knew how to ride,
Or I'd have surely been left behind.
My horse was running scared,
And through the night was running blind.

I wasn't sure which scared me most,
That eerie sound coming from the wind
Or the knowledge that my horse might kill himself
If I couldn't rein him in.

At last he ran himself out,
And slowed his pace a bit.
But still I know this is a night
We'll neither one of us forget.

I Bind Him to My Heart

With every blade and stitch of grass,
I bind him to my heart.
And every day I know with him
Is the greatest way to start.

Every shadow and every step,
We walk it side by side,
Although I nearly have to run at times
To keep up with his stride.

With every count of stock
And with every horse we straddle,
It's the two of us together
As we're tending to the cattle.

With every drop of rain
And every grain of dust,
We know our love's long lasting
Between the two of us.

With every working hour,
It seems we closer grow.
We can almost communicate
With just the thoughts we know.

Can a cowgirl have a better man
Than the one who loves her most?
And can that same cowboy
Have for himself a better host?

The Saddle

The saddle told the story
As it sat there on the rack.
It had been someone's pride and joy
Just a few years back.

It spoke of doing rodeo,
A circuit of twelve long years,
When at times its owner
Had to swallow back his fears.

It spoke of rangeland riding,
Rope burns along its horn and sides
From cattle caught and branded,
Or pulled from bogs along his rides.

Scrape marks cut the swells and fenders
From brush he'd ridden through,
And from the starlit trails
They'd ridden together too.

A bad burn across the cantle
Where a bull had run his flank,
And hit the end of the rope
And gave a taut rope yank.

The leg caught beneath the rope
Was severed to the bone:
A bad day for the rider,
Although he made it home.

The saddle proudly ridden
Through events and rain and wind.
A cowboy now one-legged,
With memories of "back then."

The saddle sits in the store.
The sign reads, For Sale.
Perhaps the price is right for someone
Who knows the saddle has its tale.

Who's the Greatest Cowboy?

Who's the greatest cowboy?
Can you give his name?
Why do you favor just him?
Did he make the Hall of Fame?

The greatest cowboy on earth
Is the one you already know,
The one who does his chores each day
And doesn't have to put on a show.

He gets up early every morning,
A way before breakfast time.
He may saddle his favorite horse,
And upon it he may climb.

Or he may grab up the pickup keys
For the work he needs to do.
And he may be gone all day
Before he gets home to you.

His kids grow up learning early
How to keep the ranch intact.
They're wiser than the city kids;
I know that for a fact.

They may grumble some,
Like any kid might do,
But to actually go bad—
There's really very few.

Their cowboy dad has brought them up
On horses of their own.
They help with sortin' cattle,
And sometimes suffer a broken bone.

They grow up knowin' how to fence
And how to mow the hay,
And how to still have manners
At the end of their long day.

He may not be related,
This cowboy whom you know.
But any way you stack it up,
He's the greatest cowboy you know.

He may not herald much fame
Or have ridden in a local rodeo,
But he'll still have a bunch of rides
In the places he will go.

He's out there on the prairie
Ridin' through brush and mesquite,
Or along ravines and streams,
Or other places where cattle cheat.

He's that man with the lariat,
Or a branding iron in his hand.
And all day long he works hard,
Your favorite cowboy man.

He may not be in movies,
But he well deserves his place
When we sit down at the table
And he says the evening grace.

Morning Ride

I'll saddle up one more time
To ride through the morning mist,
To feel the chill of the morning air
As my bare face is kissed.

I'll watch another sunrise
With its pink and light of blue,
And watch the morning sun as it bathes itself
In golden rays that seem daily new.

I'll watch a few white morning clouds
Drift lazily across the sky.
I'll make a mental note
Of everything that's caught my eye.

I'll remember these in later years,
When grandkids marvel then
At all the things this old hide
Can then relate to them.

Boots Aren't Made for Walkin'

Boots aren't made for walkin'.
That lesson has a way of coming through,
More so on days like the day
My mustang threw a shoe.

Walking was not my idea of travel,
But it was the only recourse.
I had to get back to the ranch
And get another horse.

It seemed like it took all day,
With the horse stepping gingerly behind.
The trail I chose to take
Seemed like a long thin line.

Long before I reached the ranch
My feet began to ache.
And I knew somewhere down the trail
We'd have to take a break.

Noon found me at the corral;
A new mount I had caught.
And a trip to the cookshack
Entered into my thought.

Then I was back on the range,
And as the afternoon wore on,
My thoughts drifted back to
The boots that I had on.

No sir! Boots aren't made for walkin'.
That will make itself known to you,
Just like it did to me
The day my mustang threw a shoe.

The Poker Game

We all looked at each other
As our newest member set in
On a table dealin' poker
Where we all knew he couldn't win.

A smirk went around the table
As the gamblers cast their thoughts aloft.
They figured he didn't know one card from another,
This youngster known as Croft.

But he settled into the chair quite easily,
And picked up the cards dealt to him.
He placed a bet in the center of the table
As his gaze took in all of them.

The bets went around the table.
They knew this kid was broke.
He couldn't last too long;
His playing was just a joke.

They "seen" and "raised" and had a ball,
All at this kid's expense.
He shouldn't be at a poker table;
He should be out ridin' fence.

They figured he'd get discouraged,
And in his cards he'd toss.
The game was "one-eyed jacks or better,"
And the table paid his cost.

The night wore on; the hours passed.
The cards were dealt time and time again.
Perhaps it was beginner's luck
That helped this boy win.

A king-high royal flush won a hand,
And aces yet another.
He beat a pair with jacks and treys,
And the gamblers looked at each other.

One gambler then stacked the deck
To give the kid an uneven break.
But even then his luck still held;
The kitty was his to take.

In due time he rose and said,
"Gents, I've enjoyed this, ya know,
But it's almost morning now,
And fellas, I've got to go."

I asked him on the way to the ranch,
'Cause I really had to know,
"Do you really know your cards that well,
Or was it mostly luck and blow?"

"I knew when I sat down, old-timer,
That I would take the lot.
They took me for a foolish kid,
And now they know I'm not.

"Next time they'll be more careful
If I sit in on their game.
And then if I should lose to them,
I'll be the one to blame."

What Do You Mean I Can't Be a Cowgirl?

What do you mean I can't be a cowgirl?
Just because I don't wear jeans?
At least these jodhpurs I have on
Ain't splittin' at the seams!

And so what if my ropin' skills
Are nearly next to none?
I know I can learn to rope,
And it surely looks like fun.

What? … Saddle my own horse?
That's what I thought you guys did!
What's that smart remark?
What's that you just said?

Well, I'll show you, buster!
I can ride, I know I can.
What makes you think you're better—
Just because you're a man?

What was that you said?
Do I know how to brand a cow?
Now you know I'm from the city,
And you know I don't know how.

But I can learn. I give you that.
And a cowgirl I will be.
You just sit back and watch me, buster,
'Cause you're just gonna see!

Oh, I don't wear my Stetson right,
And what would I do out in the rain?
Well, you're supposed to be the cowboy—
What do you use for brains?

What do you mean I can't be a cowgirl?
Just because I'm a city dude?
I thought cowboys were gentlemen,
But, mister, you're downright rude!

But I will be a cowgirl!
You'll see before I'm through.
And if I don't do another thing in life,
I'll live to outdo you!

Praises for the Cowgirl

Praises for the cowgirl
Tend to be a scant few.
Most folk don't realize
The day a cowgirl goes through.

She's up in the morning
Fixing breakfast for her man.
And shortly thereafter
She'll be his right hand.

Whether building a new fence
Or helping out to brand,
She'll be right there
Doing whatever she can.

She helps move the cattle
And helps with the count,
And does it afoot,
Or with the help of her mount.

She helps with the doctoring,
And helps with the hay,
And helps with the birthing
Of a newborn on the way.

She rarely complains,
Even when she's hurt.
And it's usually something she can bind
With a piece from the tail of her shirt.

And just like her man,
She gets dirty for sure,
And even sometimes slips
On a fresh mound of manure.

Sometimes there's hard feelings
From a stream of outbursts.
But she still loves her man,
Even at his worst.

She drags home in the evening,
Knowing that he's tired too.
And she fixes his meal
When their showers are through.

She may hum a tune
Or sing softly at times.
Or it may be him
Who'll make up the rhymes.

Their evenings together
Make up for it all.
And cowgirls everywhere
Deserve praises from all.

The Old Man

He sat in the same old chair
He'd sat in many weeks,
Where the warm winds whispered to him
And the sunshine kissed his cheeks.

A stray dog lay beside him.
Now and then it wagged its tail,
As if to befriend the old man,
Who seemed to be so frail.

The checkerboard beckoned
A player to come join him in a game.
But most knew how good he was
And made excuses, however lame.

Most just greeted him, "Hey there!"
I doubt they knew his name.
And no one seemed to know
From where this old man came.

And then one morning the sun rose
To find an empty chair.
The old man had disappeared,
And there was no one to care.

The Wild Mustang

He found the mustangs one afternoon
In a remote meadow near the ranch.
He spotted one he'd like to own,
If there was a prayer of a chance.

He rode there every day
And spent a little time,
And after a few trips
They didn't seem to mind.

Then he began to sing to them
As they milled around to graze.
Gradually he eased toward them,
And began to talk words of praise.

They seemed to like the talking,
Or maybe they understood
He just loved to be among them,
And would love to catch one if he could.

Then one day the one he liked
Came toward him to check him out.
It nuzzled his hand,
But it still had some doubt.

Still, that was a start.
His heart beat a tune.
And he knew right then
The colt would be his soon.

Others grazed close by,
Though the stallion kept his guard.
But none of them threatened him
As he gentled down his future pard.

Time was on his side,
And the horse also seemed to be.
It had to be the colt's decision
To no longer roam the pastures free.

He took his time with the halter,
And with teaching the horse to lead.
And he was careful with the saddle;
To spook the others was not a need.

He worked with the colt;
Time, it seemed, stood still.
The colt appeared not to mind
When the saddle he could feel.

Then one day he mounted him
And felt the thrill of that great feat.
And the colt himself seemed to think
The rider's being there was neat.

He never tried to buck
Like the cowboy expected him to.
So he started training him
To know what he must do.

No one trains a wild mustang
Without a corral or round pen.
To do it on the open range—
His pride swelled deep within.

He had gentled down the mustang,
And trained him to be ridden.
But every time he tells his tale,
Someone says, "Man, you've got to be kiddin'!"

He Never Returned

He walked down the alley slow.
In short, he put on quite a show,
Carefully picking every step
So as not to disturb those who slept.

A little swagger in his stride,
His six guns tied to either side.
His hat swept back from his face,
His eyes scanning every raunchy place.

At last the boardwalk came into view.
He stood there a minute or two
Before softly stepping onto its breadth
And pausing there a moment to rest.

The batwings of a nearby saloon
Almost brought him to his doom.
Smoke reeked from the blazing guns
Of a man retreating on the run.

Then in his back he felt a poke,
And seconds later a voice spoke.
"You're under arrest for what you done,
So move slowly and give me your gun."

He answered, "I haven't done a thing."
But his wrists fit the handcuff rings.
"Shut up and head toward the jail.
That's your new home. There'll be no bail."

But jail was not where he planned to stay.
He knew he had to get away.
Without giving a thought to what he'd done,
He'd shoved the man, and into the alley run.

He no longer put on quite a show—
Just ran and looked for a place to go,
Someplace where he could get away
So he'd not be hanged the following day

For someone else's mode of play—
The someone else who got away.
He ran, not caring whom he might wake,
For his own life was then at stake.

His followers quit that summer night
As soon as he was out of sight.
He kept on going—he never turned around.
And he never returned to that prairie town.

No more alleys did he swagger through
When in a town where he was new.
He didn't like the "by your leave"
To have to flee like a fugitive.

He never returned to that prairie town,
Where he one night had been a clown,
Where someone else's mode of play
Had nearly ended his own sweet day.

It Took a Boy

It took a boy your heart to win,
To share your love deep within.
Does he know his luck, this cherished lad,
And the kind of a man he now calls Dad?

To whom with trusting heart he looks
To help him with life and its hooks and crooks?
His seed will sprout from the love you give.
Whatever you teach him, that's how he'll live.

So teach him well, and of God's love, too,
So he can lean on God, as well as on you.
And when your temper flares back up a tad,
Remember that he's young; he's just a lad.

When his moments are colored in gray and blue,
Let him know he can lean on you.
Be there for him no matter what.
Let him know what kind of a dad he's got.

There'll be times he'll worry you,
Either from illness or the things he'll do.
But he has to learn, this precious lad,
The things that are right and the things that are bad.

And though you give him things your money can buy,
There's one thing you can't give no
matter how much you try.
For a dad can't replace a mother's care,
And a lad needs a mom's love to share.

A lad needs a mom in his darkest hour
To dote on him, her love a shower,
In whose arms he may rock,
Lessening the troubles that come to knock.

A heart filled with love can fill a boy's need
And help him sprout from a fledgling seed.
It's good to know his dad is there,
And not for a mint would he miss his care.

But the heart of a mother can burst with pride
And give him love that she can't hide.
She can do for a boy what a dad can't do
When she holds him and says, "I love you."

For a mom can give daily doses of love to his dad
And still have love to give to the lad.
I'd love to fill the void there
And share my love with the lad for whom you care.

I wish in my heart that there could be
You, the lad you love ... and me.
It took a boy your heart to win.
Is there room for a mother to come in?

The Dying Soldier's Letter

I'm writing this letter to you, Mom,
With tears in my eyes.
I don't know for sure
How much of war you can visualize.

Dad will understand, I know,
Because he's been there before
On war's mighty battleground,
Where killing's done by the score.

He'll understand that this morning
There were others next to me,
And tonight I am the last of us
Who fought today to keep us free.

Bryan stepped on a land mine;
He's scattered all over the land.
And later Jimmy lost an arm,
The one with his writing hand.

Chester caught a bullet
That dropped him instantly.
And Jordan caught some shrapnel.
He died beside me.

I know that I may die here
As I wait for more of our men.
By the time they get here,
I may be dead by then.

The noise has kind of quieted down—
Or maybe it's just me.
The paper's kind of blurring,
And I can barely see.

The wounds I have received
Are causing a good deal of pain.
So please forgive my tears, Mom,
Even though they fall in vain.

*   *   *

Just know that you and Dad
Were in these thoughts of mine,
As in my final moments here on earth,
Your son lies here dying.

He was alive when we first reached him,
And I know this sounds absurd:
He handed me this letter, then he smiled,
And he died without a word.

I didn't have the heart to tell his folks
What his letter didn't say—
That he'd written his letter to them
With half his body blown away.

And though he didn't get it said,
They know he loved them just the same.
He could have been any other soldier
By any other name.

For soldiers do write their kinfolk,
And carry nightmares evermore,
If they live to make it home to loved ones
After the horrors of the war.

But often, like this soldier,
They only get things partly said
In the letters to their loved ones,
Before they end up dead.

Those Golden Country Memories

Golden country memories
Are as fine as silver hair.
They reflect the living past
With when and why and where.

Golden country memories …
A treasury that can't be bought,
Because they contain every little detail
And every little thought.

Golden country memories
To enjoy when I'm old.
Of times and places and happenings
That no other could have told.

Golden country memories
That privately are only mine,
That I can reflect back upon
At any given time.

Golden country memories,
In memory they're preserved—
The ones that brought me happiness,
And some I thought were undeserved.

Golden country memories,
If written in a book,
Would not matter enough for most
To pick it up and have a look.

Golden country memories
With which I have been blessed
Are recorded in my mind
As though they were a request.

Golden country memories
That put my life to a test,
They'll be with me all my life
Until I am laid to rest.

The Silent Hills

They gave my heart many joyous thrills,
Those ever-beckoning silent hills.
Down below, yet safe and sound,
The canyons cut into the ground.

And ever narrow, or deep and wide,
Breathtaking valleys choose to hide.
Little streams flowing freely, too,
Blend their color with heaven's blue.

The beauty of the setting sun
When at last the day is done,
Casting shadows along the mountain's might,
Is at best a stunning sight.

And with the coming of the dawn,
They'll be feeding, both doe and fawn.
Hear the singing of the morning fowl
As nature's own begin to prowl.

The lifting of the morning fog
Blankets the quiet mountain dialogue.
While you're still there,
Breathe deeply of the mountain air.

Then the sun shall rise again
To release the beauty remaining within,
The grasp of grandeur that is ever instilled
In those ever-beckoning silent hills.

Don't Trip over a Snowflake

Large snowflakes were coming down,
Covering everything in sight.
They seemed to be just everywhere
As they pelted through the daylight.

I stepped out among them,
And thought I heard a voice say,
"Don't trip over a snowflake
While you're out there today."

One landed on my cheek
And melted down my face,
Leaving a trail of wet
As another took its place.

So slowly they came down,
And they melted right away.
"Don't trip over a snowflake
While you're out there today."

They were alighting on my jacket
And getting in my hair.
"Don't trip over a snowflake
Today while you're out there."

I brushed them from my sleeve
And brushed them from my face,
And marveled as they fell
At their size and at their grace.

I went ahead and did the chores,
And then when I was through,
I wondered at the voice.
I'd heard it, this I knew.

As I brushed the snowflakes from my coat
And brushed them from my eyes,
I heard that voice again,
Much to my surprise.

"Don't trip over a snowflake,"
It told me one more time.
"Those snowflakes are beautiful,
And all of them are Mine."

A Cowboy's Testimony

The cowboy gave his testimony;
His soul he hoped to redeem.
He told us of the night Jack Daniels
Met John Three Sixteen.

He told us how he'd had to choose
Between his Bible and his drink,
And how a voice had asked him
How much lower he could sink.

He'd lived his life the Devil's way,
And gloried in its wrath,
Until the day the Lord took ahold of him
And showed him a different path.

As a man he'd had his failings,
And whiskey was the comfort he reached for
When life had handed him hard times,
And his family had shown him the door.

Whiskey had been the friend he knew.
It let him face each day.
But tonight the Bible was there
To guide him on his way.

With trembling hands he lifted
The Bible from where it lay.
He read the passage and tried to interpret
What John Three Sixteen had to say.

"For God so loved the world ..."
Those words he read aloud.
As he finished the passage,
His eyes began to cloud.

As he laid the Bible down,
Its pages fell open to Psalm 23,
Where everlasting life was his
As he read on through verse three.

The decision wasn't easy
For the cowboy on that night,
But he put away a life of sin
And asked God to set him right.

That night he made a friend
And knew on God he could lean.
He had no more use for Jack Daniels.
He'd found a friend in John Three Sixteen.

The Rancher and the Salesman

The man pulled the surrey to a stop
In front of the main ranch house.
He hailed the boss and then said to him,
"I thought cowboys only worked with cows."

The owner grinned at the newcomer
And, deciding to have a little fun,
Said, "I had to hire me some farmhands
To get some of this work done."

The visitor was a salesman;
To sell some insurance was what he tried.
But these were just temporary farmhands,
To the salesman the rancher lied.

"And that pasture full of cattle
That maybe you took as prime—
Those belong to my neighbors.
Very few of them are mine.

"You see, I've got a banker
That I keep trying to duck.
I couldn't afford your insurance
Even if you sold it for a buck."

The insurance man raised his eyes
And looked across the way.
He noted the "temporary" farmhands,
And then he drove away.

The Razorback Hog

The old man's name was Larry,
And he liked to talk a lot.
Every now and then he'd tell
About the hog that put him in a spot.

He loved to hunt the old razorbacks.
He hunted them just for fun,
Until he ran across the one
That cost him his new gun.

He claims he never heard the hog
That slipped up on him from behind.
He could only beat it off with his gun,
Until he could find a tree to climb.

And as he dropped the gun
To climb into the tree,
The hog ripped his left leg
From his ankle to his knee.

Some hours later the hog got bored,
And finally left Larry alone.
Finally he could come down from the tree
And drag his injured body home.

He doesn't hunt the razorbacks
Like he used to, just for fun.
He thinks about it here and there,
And then remembers what that last hog done.

The Pond

The trees threw their shadows
Out across the pond.
The tree was old and ancient
That I leaned upon.

The birds called to each other
And flew from branch to branch.
I could name many of them,
As most were residents of the ranch.

Here and there a turtle
Brought its head up for air.
I really don't know
How many turtles and frogs live there.

Water striders scurried
Across the water there,
And it seemed like dragonflies
Were dipping everywhere.

Now and then a fish
Swam lazily near the shore.
I watched these activities
Until I could watch no more.

Your Daddy Has Just Retired

Has your daddy given up
The life he loved the best?
Has he actually retired from
His dream, his childhood quest?

Is that his bridle hanging there,
That leather he carried with him everywhere?
And is that your daddy's saddle
Slung across the saddle rest?

And those are his leather chaps
He's hung there with the rest.
And alongside all of that,
He hung his leather vest.

Up there on the nails
Hang the irons he branded with.
It isn't like your daddy
To give up things like this.

But age has caught up with him,
And although it nearly makes me cry,
I'll never question his decision—
No, I'll never ask him why.

I know he'll count on you, son,
To carry on the life he loved the best.
Yes, he's left it all for you, son,
And he knows you'll do your best.

Deflated Dreams

He rode the rail to Memphis:
Song City, USA.
Folks had told him he could sing,
And he meant to have his day.

As he walked the streets of Memphis,
His dream began to deflate.
It seemed like everywhere he went,
He got there a few years too late.

"Country singers come and go."
That's mostly what they said.
As he walked, he thought
Of the singing life he'd led.

Singing around the campfires,
Singing for the wife and kids.
Singing now and then in bars
When he could get the bid.

The bench along the park side
Offered him a seat.
He took it because by now
He was really beat.

A few minutes he just sat there,
Then he picked up his guitar.
His mind blocked out all else;
In those moments he was a singing star.

There were people standing around him
When he came out of his reverie.
They told him to go to Nashville;
That's where he needed to be.

He played the weekend in a bar,
Compliments of his new friends.
But at last he boarded the train for home.
His dreams he'd have to mend.

An Autumn Evening

He was slouched in his chair,
Resting his feet on the rail,
Relaxing with his harmonica
And tunes of the trail.

The summer was now past
And fall was setting in,
With colored leaves on trees
Every now and then.

Some were on the ground
Playing with the breeze,
Which picked them up gently
And sent them floating along with ease.

The cattle were fattened now
Against winter's oncoming abuse.
And new hay bales were drying
In the fields for his winter use.

Winter wheat was planted
In straight and even rows.
It would help feed the cattle
When spring brought winter's close.

Crickets here and there were chirping,
And a frog croaked now and then,
Lending voices to the world
As evening began to descend.

The wail of a coyote
Somewhere in the distance
Warned the whole countryside
Of that clan's existence.

The hoot of an owl
Broke in now and then
From wherever he was perched
On some nearby tree limb.

The mare snickered softly
To the foal by her side,
As behind a cloud
The sun began to hide.

The harmonica blended into the evening
Along with all the rest.
That this rancher was tired,
One would never guess.

He sat slouched in his chair,
Resting his feet upon the rail,
Relaxing with his harmonica
And the tunes of the trail.

A Winter's Day

So fresh the air with its morning chill,
And the wind itself today is still.
Mounding up in glistening glow
Is the freshly fallen drifting snow.

Icicles drip from every tree,
With rainbows of prisms sparkling free—
An awesome sight for all to see,
The sight that quietly beckons me.

A beauty only God could cast,
Serenity while yet it lasts.
Not a mark on its unscarred face;
Not a footprint can be traced.

Dare I disturb this quiet glow
And plant my feet onto the snow,
Where my footprints will have marred
A mournful crunch into the yard?

But if I am to do my work,
I cannot my duties shirk.
In spite of the beauty that I see,
There are those who depend on me.

A winter's day that God bequeathed,
Another treasure He unleashed.
A memory I will tuck away:
The beauty of this, a winter's day.

The Old Preacher

He walked bent over in his suit of brown.
He was the only preacher we had in our town.
He knew the townsfolk as well as old Doc did.
It seemed he was old when I was just a kid.

He strolled the countryside every once in a while.
He knew every inch of every square mile.
He met every stranger who set foot in our town.
And every now and then I'd see him drink a round.

The blackjack table offered him an occasional chair.
The guns in his holsters had business being there.
But come Sunday morning at the prayer meeting hall,
There was standing room only, even outside the walls.

He preached every sermon in a language they all knew,
And in a tone of voice they could all adhere to.
They gave their tithes, no matter how poor.
And they all shook his hand as they came out the door.

I was too young to fully understand
How great he was, this old preacher man.
He's long since left us for a home up above,
But he's still talked about in tones filled with love.

Christmas at the Line Shack

I found a big old pinecone
That had fallen from a tree.
I set it in the middle of the table
To use as a Christmas tree.

There weren't any ornaments to put on it
'Cause the line shack's far from town,
And out here in this wilderness,
There just ain't too much layin' around.

I shot me a snowshoe rabbit.
It's sizzling while it cooks.
And I found some wild onions
Down yonder by the brook.

I'll stir me up some biscuits
And dream of Grandma's apple pie.
And I'll turn the rabbit over
And let the other side of him fry.

I lucked upon some hickory nuts
And a tree of chinquapins.
Never thought I'd be eating acorns;
Thought only squirrels ate them.

I went out and fed the horses,
And made sure they all drank.
I'm not so sure that in the wintertime
Those horses don't pull rank.

But what the heck … it's Christmas Eve
Up here at this line shack,
And snow has started falling
As I carry myself on back.

I picked up a pile of wood
And brought it inside with me.
We'll have us a good Christmas;
My pinecone "tree" and me.

I think of old Christmas carols
Like my mother used to sing,
And peacefulness descends on me
Like a bird on the wing.

It's just a few more hours now
Until it will be Christmas Day.
But up here in this line shack,
It'll be another day to pray.

Cowboy Snowmen

Because the snow had covered the land,
I did what most folks do:
I built myself a snowman
While the snow was fresh and new.

Because he was bare,
I left him there
While I went in search of
Some old worn discarded stuff.

An old battered hat I found,
And a pipe, old and cracked.
A scarf with a couple of snags,
And one old gunnysack.

I put the hat upon his head,
And the scarf around his neck.
I stuck the pipe in his mouth,
And back to the house I crept.

I searched for more things to use
On the snowman I had made,
When a glow came through the window
And lighted up the shade.

I went to the window,
And there in my front yard,
My snowman was busy
Makin' himself a pard!

As I watched him work,
I stared on aghast ...
Before he was through, out on my lawn,
There sat a dozen matched!

And then I heard music begin,
And those snowmen began to sing.
And as they sang, they worked ...
And horses sprang into being.

I swear I saw a herd of steers
Cross my driveway there.
It seemed to me they bawled
And came from everywhere.

I'd surely be trampled if I ran outside.
I could only stand and stare.
I couldn't move from that one spot.
It seemed I was frozen there.

But don't you know those cowboys
Rode those horses they'd created,
And pretty soon they'd turned that herd,
And the stampede was soon abated.

All were dressed in cowboy garb,
And they rode those horses well.
They turned those critters they had chased
Back into that snowbound dale.

The snowmen then gathered in a circle.
No campfire for their plight.
As each found a place to sit,
Their singing filled the night.

Then soon I saw them take the snow,
And the instruments they'd made,
And on into the night they sang,
And on those instruments played.

Happy snowmen cowboys,
A true sight to behold
As they sat in my front yard
On a winter night so cold.

I know I must be cracking up,
Or losing sanity.
There sat a dozen snowmen,
And only one belonged to me.

A memory I will wonder about
In long hours yet to come.
And I'll probably wonder also
Why I never kept it mum.

Twenty Feet Tall

In memory of Joe Smoot of Laverne, Oklahoma

When I first met you,
I was pretty small.
I remember asking you
If you were twenty feet tall.

You always had a twinkle in your eyes
And a smile on your face.
I grew up around you,
With you all around the place.

You were in and out of my life,
Like the warm winds that blew.
I never gave a thought
To a life without you.

You were like a favorite pup,
Or like a favorite horse.
You were just sort of there
As life ran its course.

You had medals from the war;
You'd served in the Philippines.
But I was just a little girl,
Barely more than a toddler in jeans.

You gave out your love,
Probably much more than your share.
And you asked nothing in return
For showing us you cared.

You had read the Bible at least six times.
Its pages were tattered and worn.
You probably knew it better than most,
For you read it both evening and morn.

It just never registered
That one day you'd not be there,
That God would one day call you home
And place you under His care.

Many came to your funeral …
They came from far and near.
There must have been at least a hundred,
And not one dry tear.

The pastor committed your soul
To God in front of us all.
As I brushed away a tear, Joe …
You're still twenty feet tall.

How Lucky I Have Been

How lucky I have been
To have lived in a time
When people cared for others
And there was no selfish "mine";

When a person's word
And handshake was worthy of note.
We could trust the bond one carried proudly;
It needed no legal note.

How lucky I have been
That I was taught the way
To share in other people's needs
And to kneel with them to pray.

It was a time when a thank-you was full payment
For whatever deeds were rendered there
By respectful friends and neighbors
Who took the time to care.

In the Midst of This Storm

I'm driving cattle home
Against driving wind and snow.
A chore for me and my horse,
Because they don't want to go.

It comes through so naturally—
The howling of the wind,
Which drives the cold
To the bone marrow within.

The cold stings my eyes,
Their corners filling with tears.
Aggravation sets in
As I try to drive these steers.

The horse doesn't like it
Any better than me,
But we've got to drive them in;
They have to be fed, you see.

Fences they have crossed
Over tops of frozen snowdrifts.
It's been a long time
Since I've seen drifts like this.

The cattle don't like being driven
Against this wind and snow.
But the worst of it is over;
We've not too far to go.

Then they'll get some hay,
And they'll also get some cake.
I'll put my horse and me inside,
And get rid of some of this ache.

But out here while I'm riding
In the midst of this storm,
I'm beginning to wonder
If I'll ever get warm.

His Horse

He made his brag to me
About his horse,
How it ran from him
And he'd had to rope it, of course.

He entered the corral;
He had something to prove.
It stood and let him come to it.
Rare—but the horse didn't move.

I entered the corral—
A natural thing to do.
I petted his gelding,
And I talked to it too.

He stood like a statue,
Beauty in his own right,
Not moving a muscle,
Nor moving in fright,

But taking in loving
From this female hand.
And when I left the corral,
He continued to stand.

His master asked me
What I had done to his horse.
I gave him something to think about:
That's what I did to the horse.

It needed to stop running from Master
And playing that silly game
Of making his master rope him
Whenever he came.

His master loves him,
To the horse I had explained.
And he's an expert roper;
He doesn't need to be trained.

He loves his master,
And of him he needs to take care,
For there may be a day
When Master won't be there.

His master thinks horses
Don't know what you say,
But he never again had to rope his horse
After my talk with him that day.

One Memory of Champ

I thought again tonight
Of the paint I used to ride
And of the times when I was sick
And he never left my side.

If I slipped from the saddle,
Too sick to ride on him,
Why, he'd kneel down beside me
Until I could mount again.

If I caught ahold of the latigo
And stumbled with every step,
He'd slow his step to match mine,
And his vigil on me he kept.

He snickered every now and then,
And reached back to nudge me too,
As if to say, *It's all right, Jan,
I'm gonna see you through.*

Funny how one thinks of these things
When her favorite mount is gone
And there's nothing left but memories
That she can draw upon.

The Water Well

I was just a youngster.
Why, I couldn't even spell.
But I can remember drinking water
Out of the old water-drawn well.

We didn't have filters back then
To keep out little bits of debris.
Why, Pop just drew a cup and drink,
And then hand the cup to me.

We kept a bucket full of water
I'd always heard was "just in case."
But when that water came out of that well,
You just couldn't find any better taste.

We hadn't ever heard of fluoride,
Or that other thing called chlorine.
And we didn't know there were germs—
Those are things we'd never seen.

That water came from that well
As cool as it could be,
And it came from down inside the earth,
Where the water bills are free.

Not a sweeter taste could e'er be found,
As far as Pop and I were concerned,
Than the water drawn from the ground.
Thank goodness we were both unlearned!

The Cowgirl

The guys all thought it was funny
That a girl should want to ride.
They used to taunt and tease,
And do their best to chide.

But when she roped the steed,
And put her saddle on,
And slipped the bridle over his head,
Some of their smiles were gone.

They didn't think a girl
Could mount a horse like a man.
They stood in idle wonder
When she showed them that she can.

They expected then to see
This cowgirl lapping up some dust.
They knew this horse would throw her,
And her backside she would bust.

But she held onto him firmly
While he pitched a time or two,
And left the guys regarding her
From a different point of view.

Country Girl, Go Home

You have just moved into the city,
But you're just a simple country girl.
You don't know the ways of the big city.
It's not your back-home kind of world.

Don't listen if you don't want to
To someone who's trying to be a friend,
But if you stay here in the city,
Country girl, the city will do you in.

It'll show you what it's like to be hurt
In more ways than you have ever known.
It will strip you of your pride, girl,
And you'll find your soul is not your own.

The city is filled with the kinds of evil
That will prey upon your trusting heart.
And the sin and shame it will pawn off on you
Will tear the morals that you have all apart.

When you've reached the depths of the gutter,
And you walk these city streets all alone,
Maybe then you will sometimes remember,
Country girl, that I begged you to go on home.

The Artist

He sat on the ground,
His tablet in his lap.
His pencil moved rapidly,
As if afraid it might get trapped.

His mind wandered aimlessly
Amid the morning sun.
And he seemed not to notice
What his pencil there had done.

His hand moved freely.
Charcoal quickly filled the pages—
Artwork in transition—
Capturing memories upon the pages.

From his memory came
His days out on the range.
These soon became visible
As the charcoal made the change.

A rodeo bronc had thrown him.
A stage had broken down.
A river had been forded,
And a rider nearly drowned.

The charcoal charted everything
He remembered from his youth,
And brought it forth on paper—
A record of the truth.

As he rose again to his pony
And put his art away,
He realized he had imaged
His own biography today.

He frowned as he wondered
If in years to come
Anyone would appreciate
What the artist today had done.

Would they recognize a photograph
By the charcoal on the page
As the life of a cowboy,
Once he was old with age?

And then in the future,
When he and life must part,
Would they someday appreciate
The artist and his art?

The Colt

I sit on this rail
And watch him play.
He'll be big enough
To break in some day.

He's long of limb
And graceful in gait.
He holds his head high,
Like he can hardly wait

For the day to come
When, like his mom, he'll be
The one bearing the saddle
I'll have beneath me.

No fancy parades for this little guy.
No rodeos will he have to help win.
But he'll know the rangeland
And the cattle we'll bring in.

I'll train him myself
When it comes that time.
Then I'll know he's trained right
And that he'll respond in kind.

We'll be trusting each other
While working each day.
And as any rancher knows,
It can't be any other way.

Stranger in Town

He was a man who looked to me
Like a man right out of the old-time West.
What his intentions were I don't know,
And I never could have guessed.

His hat sat tilted just a little bit
On the top of his head.
It kept the sun from his eyes,
And the rain it also shed.

There was a distant look in his eyes.
His face was shallow and gaunt,
And it was tanned and weathered,
As though his life had been one of want.

His clothes were dusty
And a little worse for wear.
His shirt even supported
A small three-cornered tear.

Sleek and black was the horse he led;
I couldn't help admiring it.
It walked with pride—an animal well bred—
And I wished I owned one like it.

I asked the stranger
If he had business here to do.
He smiled and assured me
That he was just passing through.

151

Soldiers in Your Cup

He woke up early
And turned on the TV.
A commercial for Folgers coffee
Was airing for him to see.

He checked on his mom.
She was still asleep.
So back to the kitchen
The youngster then did creep.

He filled the carafe with water
And poured it into the pot.
And next a paper filter
From the bag it was in he got.

Then he got the coffee—
Was it one scoop or two?
He couldn't remember exactly
Just what he'd seen his mom do.

Just to make sure,
He dumped more coffee in,
And then he punched the button
And let the brew begin.

Then he woke his mom.
When she sat up,
He handed her the liquid
In the steaming coffee cup.

And because he had made it,
She continued to slowly drink.
But at the bottom of the cup,
She found cause to blink.

Three tiny soldiers,
Each one faceup,
Stared back at her
From the bottom of her cup.

She stared at them a moment
Before she asked of him
To please explain to her
Why they had been put in.

A grin spread across his face,
And his young eyes lit up.
"Mama, haven't you ever heard
Of waking up in the morning
With soldiers in your cup?"

The Seat That God Put There

There were no empty chairs
In the space where I stood,
But beneath the boughs of a shading elm,
There lay a pile of cut-up wood.

Most had brought their own chairs
And placed them in neat rows.
Most of those who had come
Were sitting now in those.

We were waiting by the round pen
For the revival to begin,
After which we'd watch the pastor
Ride a colt he was breaking in.

It was as though a voice whispered,
"Come, you can sit upon the wood."
It sure beat standing up,
Although there was shade there where I stood.

The wood creaked now and then
As I shifted my weight around.
But by and large it was the best,
This seat that God had found.

It was just enough above the ground
From where those other folks all sat
That I could see everything being done—
And you can't beat a deal like that.

Now and then I flicked off an ant
Who'd come to check me out,
Or maybe it just wanted a higher place
To see what the revival was all about.

God provided a gentle breeze,
So our summer evening was quite fair.
And I enjoyed the entire night,
On the seat that God put there.

The Good Old Days

I reached back with jubilation
And brought the past back to me.
I watched the horse race the wind,
Watched the flight of a little wren.

Smiled while the baby laughed.
Enjoyed the frolics of a baby calf.
Watched the jackrabbit skitter away.
Listened to the burro bray.

Watched a leaf gliding by
On the river that mirrored the sky.
Recalled many longtime friends
And things we used to try.

Pinned our hopes and future dreams
On our love and wedding rings.
Noted the serenity of the ways
Things were done in bygone days.

The good old days, we think of them,
Reflections of our living then;
Slower-paced, less violent times.
I relish the good old days of "when."

Ever Chased a Rabbit?

Have you ever chased a rabbit
Down a pasture trail,
Between the growing sage,
Sometimes scaring up some quail?

Believe me, that rabbit
Will suddenly hang a pivot turn,
And shortly you're long past him,
With a lesson you have learned.

He'll sit still in the underbrush,
His coat blending right on in,
While you sputter to yourself
About how foolishly you'd lost him.

Sometimes you can scare him up again
And further chase that hare.
But then he'll jump into a hole
That you didn't know was there.

And you're left muttering to yourself,
Though no one else might care,
That you've been outsmarted
By a creature like a hare.

If Services Are Over

He hung his spurs on his saddle horn.
His clothes were not the best,
But they were all he had to wear;
He couldn't help the way he dressed.

He walked with light footsteps
As he entered the building there.
The sermon was already over,
And their heads were bowed in prayer.

A board creaked as he stepped inside,
And some folks looked his way.
But he noted that the preacher
Continued still to pray.

When the prayer was over,
The preacher looked up and saw
The old man standing in the back
In a well-worn mackinaw.

"Services are already over," said he.
"But welcome to our house.
I don't think I've seen you before.
Did you bring your spouse?"

The cowboy removed his hat,
And though his clothes did reek,
He caught the preacher's eye
And thus began to speak.

"It's been nigh on fifty years
Since I came into the Lord's house.
And at least twenty have gone past
Since He took my spouse.

"I ain't dressed like some of you,
And of you I don't know any.
But it looks to me like
The Lord has blessed you plenty.

"But to say 'Services are over'
I think is such poor taste.
My Lord always lingers;
He never leaves in haste.

"You can look around the range anywhere,
And there the Lord's work is seen.
I'd rather live my life, friend,
Where my God is both felt and seen."

Saying such, he turned to go,
And on his way out was heard to fret:
"If services are over, Lord,
These good folks ain't found You yet."

The Water Witch

I used to think my dad
Had a mental block or two,
Whenever I would see him
Walk the yard fro and to.

He'd take the branch of a peach tree
And cut it into a Y,
And back and forth he'd walk.
I finally asked him why.

It sounded kind of corny,
Like an old wives' tale to me,
When he said he was hunting water
With the limb from that peach tree.

I laughed aloud at this.
How could it possibly be
That the place where he would dig his well
Could be found by the branch of a tree?

But as the branch bent down,
Dad marked the spot quoted by the tree.
And a few days later, much to my surprise,
His well pumped water clear and free.

With Clouds Hung Low

With the whispering winds,
And the clouds hung low,
Time seems to stand still.
It's surely moving slow.

Wonder why I'm out here—
I could be home in bed.
But here I am on horseback
Hazing cattle instead.

I guess about all that matters
Is getting them where they go,
And watching out for rain
With the clouds hung low.

They're bawling and they're milling.
It's just as if they know
There's rain on the way,
With the clouds hung low.

They have grazed this pasture down,
But there's another one yet to mow.
As we're leaving this one,
I decide that's where they'll go.

As I watch them plod along,
And count each and every head,
I know why I'm on horseback
And not home in my bed.

Performance Night

His performance was scheduled for seven o'clock.
Folks had gathered around,
Each one conversing about his drive
And where he'd be later bound.

Motels were full to overflowing.
Folks had come from near and far.
Some, of course, were local,
But most had come by car.

The performance began that night
With Mother Nature's best:
A rumble of thunder and lightning—
And friend, you know the rest.

A downpour of rain
Caught us all off guard.
And I mean to tell you, friend,
It was raining hard.

The entertainer was a popular sort,
And waiting for his time,
Was well aware of the complaining,
Some of it unrefined.

Fans wanted him out in the rain.
The clock said he was overdue.
But to stand or sit out in the rain,
Not a one of them would do.

The rain let up, but brought the cold,
And even then they stayed
To enjoy his performance,
Even though it had been delayed.

Homemade Brew

There was a time when I was young
My folks made homemade brew,
From a recipe given to them
By someone they knew.

We gathered what bottles we could find
Along the main highway.
We took them home and washed them,
And boiled them to get the germs away.

We watched the brew for many days,
Waiting for it to ferment just right.
Then came time to bottle the brew
And get the caps on tight.

My sister and my cousin joined me
In sampling this homemade brew.
We had to know if it was good enough
To be drunk by the adults too.

We had a plastic tube we stuck into the crock.
We sucked on it until the brew came through to us.
We'd squeeze the tube and pass it on,
So we didn't spill any of it on us.

It was a new taste to us female teens.
We whiled away the hours,
Never realizing that as we drank,
The brew took us into its powers.

We began to talk and laugh
As we partook of this new delight.
And when our parents found us,
We must have looked a sight!

They never made more homemade brew,
So we girls could never sip another.
I'm sure that drunken teens were not ideal
To our fathers and our mothers.

"Home-Wrecker"

He painstakingly painted
The sign on his truck.
It took him a while,
But he never gave up.

He was in need of a job,
And it surely seemed sane
To paint the tailgate
With his most recent aim.

Then when people were behind him,
On the highway or in town,
They could look no further;
Their worker was found.

They just needed to call
The phone number he gave.
And it didn't cost much
For him to be their slave.

But people drove by and pointed
And laughed as they did.
His friends were no more;
They'd all gone and hid.

Not one person had a reason
His work to doubt.
Construction he knew
Both inside and out.

The sign he had painted
Was quite a little trekker.
But how do you take a sign
That reads, "Home-Wrecker"?

The Hard-Core Man

He's known to all as a hard-core man,
But he's the most gentle man I've ever seen.
He can cowboy with the best of them
And bring those critters in from the green.

I've never seen a rope that's quite so fast
When they're branding in the draw.
It will catch the fastest steer—
That's the rope the steer never saw.

The horse he rides may not be a beauty,
But it will work all day and into the night.
And he never has to worry about it—
That horse will do him right.

Among the men he works with,
His word, though mean at times, is law.
And if they can't follow his orders,
Their wages from him they'll draw.

The men all know that from none of them
He'll never take any guff.
And if your plan is to cross him,
You'd best go pack your stuff.

They all know he'll treat them right,
In spite of his hard-core attitudes.
They'll go along with what he wants,
And they'll put up with his moods.

Pride rules him with a hand of iron;
The boss he has to be.
And out on the range, hard core
Is mostly what the men will see.

But once he steps inside our home,
I can visibly see his changes,
As love transforms him into a gentle man,
Where inside my heart he ranges.

Santa's Sleigh

We heard the news today
That Santa's sleigh was broken down.
At least that was the rumor
That made the rounds in town.

Will he find another transport
To carry the things he brings?
Will he hear the Christmas carols
That everybody sings?

Will he use his magic
To make his new transport go?
And will we hear him once again
Depart with "Ho! Ho! Ho!"?

Mom's known Santa all her life.
She said of him to me,
"Some of his gifts are stamped Priority,
And the rest are marked Special Delivery."

So on Christmas Eve,
We may not hear Santa's sleigh,
But we need not panic—
Old Santa'll be on the way.

Our Cowboy Church

What do you think of when
You think of a cowboy church?
Maybe a place out in the country
Where only cowboys go through the door.
Or perhaps you picture it standing alone
In some remote grove or moor,
Where an aging preacher fills the pew
And the congregation is but few.

Perhaps you think of a hilltop
Where cowboys stop to pray,
And gaze across the beauty
That God has sent their way.
Or maybe a gathering beneath a cottonwood's shade,
Where earlier in the week the children played.
Where they've come to remind us, as folks will do,
That God is always with us, and that He loves you too.

Our cowboy church is different—
It's a beautiful place to be,
Although I know there are those
Who would think of it differently.
Our Jesus was born in a manger
With animals all around.
Our cowboy church was born in an auction barn
Just a few miles west of town.

No painted words on bricks of red,
Not a steeple stands overhead.
A cowboy church where believers go,
And where God's Word is read.
Pastor Dan O'Daniel leads us there,
Even when we bow our heads in prayer.
The angels fill the empty seats,
And you can feel God's presence there.

Perhaps Dan's a little earthy
With his sermons now and then.
But you always know he's traveled
The Bible deep within.
An old milk pail is there to collect our dues.
Collection plates are things we never use.
Music fills the rafters from the singers we get in.
We love listening to the gospel sung to us from them.

And yes, we raise our voices,
To praise His living Word,
And care not that an auction barn
For a church is quite absurd.
A barn was good enough for Jesus,
And it was good enough for His Dad.
So, we invite you to our cowboy church.
When you leave here, that you came here you'll be glad.

**Lucky's Shadowbar- a beautiful Appaloosa
stallion once owned by Janice N. Chapman.**

Writin' the Range reflects the timeless struggles of life in the American West. It depicts the honest struggle and triumph of yesteryear, and of today in some parts of the West, and remembers in part the making of the western United States. It offers a well-rounded portrait both of the cowboy life and of the everyday country folks who call cattle country their home.

Among those who encouraged me to write country-related poems were the late Louis Carle, the late Rod Nichols, the late Doc Stovall, Eddy Harrison, R. W. Hampton, Barry Ward, Baxter Black, Ron Brinegar, Jerry Nine, Verlin Pitt, Harvey Derrick, Stan Paregein, Hal Swift, and a host of other folks.

ABOUT THE AUTHOR

Chrystal with Janice N. Chapman

Janice N. Chapman was born in Woodward, Oklahoma, on December 25, 1941. She grew up on a farm southwest of Laverne, Oklahoma.

Her poetry, both fiction and fact, reflects the emotions of the people of that area, the love, the losses, the hardships, the joys. Other books she has written include *Priceless Pages from Amazing People*, *If I Could Be a Poet*, and—one western novel—*Destiny's Call*. She currently lives in Harper, Kansas, where she owns the Prairie Angel Thrift Shop. She also has Jan's House of Values, at http://janshouseofvalues.xyz.

Printed in the United States
By Bookmasters